# MANCHESTER FROM THE AIR

# MANCHESTER FROM THE AIR

WEBBAVIATION.CO.UK

breedon books
PUBLISHING

First published in Great Britain in 2007 by

The Breedon Books Publishing Company Limited

Breedon House, 3 The Parker Centre,

Derby, DE21 4SZ.

Reprinted 2009

ISBN 978-1-85983-734-4


Printed and bound in China by 1010 Printing International Ltd.

## Acknowledgements

There are many people who have helped in the making of this book, and I would like to express particular thanks to the following: John Seville, the UK's best photo pilot whose skill in placing the aircraft precisely where it is required must be telepathic; the long suffering National Air Traffic Control Service at Manchester airport, who are always helpful in squeezing a photo detail between the airliners; fellow aerial photographers Catherine Wheildon and William Cross for their friendship, support and stress counselling.

# Contents

Introduction

Manchester is a fascinating city and is currently undergoing a boom, the like of which it has not experienced since it pioneered the Industrial Revolution. The subjects I have photographed range from the Roman fort at Castlefield to the very latest cutting-edge architecture such as the Imperial War Museum at Salford Quays and the Beetham Tower. The area is a lively, modern urban conurbation but still contains historical gems from the distant past, such as the 15th-century buildings at the Chetham's School of Music. When choosing the geographical boundaries of this book, I decided to ignore the political divisions and simply chose the boundary most visible from the air, the M60 ring road. Thus the contents include Manchester, Salford and the suburbs up to and including the ring road. It is an interesting historical fact that, although Manchester has tended to dominate the area in recent years, in previous centuries it was Salford that was the major town. In the last six years, though, Salford has started to catch up, and the Quays area is a model for the regeneration of an area.

**Pages 8 and 9:** Barton Aerodrome, Britain's first municipal airport, with the city centre in the background. The aerodrome is the location of the world's oldest operational control tower and acts as the base for most of my flying.

Suburban

## Ancoats

This typical Mancunian terraced housing is so evocative of the Ancoats area of the city, which was the world's first industrial suburb. This area was once known as 'Little Italy' due to the large number of Italian immigrants living there in the 19th century. It is now a conservation area and is being extensively redeveloped, and thanks to local preservation groups many of the fine 18th and 19th-century buildings, such as St Peter's Church and Murrays' Mill complex, are being restored and given new uses. Prominent in the above photograph is the *Daily Express* building: one of Manchester's most striking buildings, with its black glass and 1930s art-deco architecture.

**Previous page:** Platt Fields Park and Fallowfield with Wilbraham Road in the foreground, looking across Moss Side towards the city centre.

## Ardwick

In recent years Manchester has undergone a great deal of regeneration, and large parts of the city have been reconstructed entirely. The images above and left show the Grove Village project. The estate has been remodelled with new housing, three neighbourhood parks and a new village centre to provide modern urban living. The work has involved the demolition of over 400 houses and construction of over 600 new houses, together with the refurbishment of another 600 properties. The remodelled layout features a new 'Green Route' through the estate, to provide a green and safe route for motorists, which features traffic calming measures and recreational areas along the way.

**Overleaf:** Moston and north-east Manchester.

## Moss Side

**Above:** Alexandra Park was opened in 1870 and was one of the first public parks in the city. The oval on the right was originally constructed to house a cricket pitch, and then later a bandstand was built. In this picture the dry ground of summer shows up a circle in the grass, in the centre of which the bandstand once stood.

**Right:** Maine Road, Moss Side. Once home to the Manchester City football ground, all that now remains is the outline of the stadium, while its replacement can be seen in the background at the top of the photograph. The Maine Road area is due to be redeveloped with new houses.

## Platt Fields Park

Platt Fields Park was originally a private estate but was later bought and redeveloped by Manchester Corporation and opened as a public park on 7 May 1910. Its most impressive feature is the man-made lake which covers over six acres and can be seen for a considerable distance from the air. The park has been a popular venue for a variety of events over the years, including the Manchester Flower Show.

## Prestwich

**This page:** A parade marches down Bury New Road in Prestwich, while the funfair is in full swing in St Mary's Park, below.

**Right:** This is a wide angle view of Prestwich taken from above the River Irwell, with the Prestwich Golf Course on the centre-right of the photograph. In the lower right-hand corner is the Cussons factory where they make Imperial Leather Soap.

## Princess Road

Princess Road at its intersection with Platt Lane, Fallowfield. After World War Two, large parts of Manchester were rebuilt to replace bomb-damaged and slum housing. These new council estates were intended to provide quality housing for working people and have proved much more successful than the high-rise experiments of the 1960s and 70s.

## Salford

**Above:** Flats on Cannon Street, Salford. The City of Salford is often overshadowed by Manchester, but historically it was Salford that was the key town, with Manchester being just a part of what was once called Salfordshire, which covered most of what is now Greater Manchester. The area is now thriving, with the regenerated Salford Quays and a strong student population attending the university there.

**Left:** Half Edge Lane, Eccles, with the M602 motorway on the right of the image taking traffic into Manchester.

## St Marys and Whitworth Park

**Above:** St Mary's Hospital for Women and Children was founded in 1790 and is still a key asset today within the Central Manchester Healthcare Trust. It is also part of a £250 million reconstruction project.

**Right:** Whitworth Park was built as a memorial to Sir Joseph Whitworth, the famous engineer, and was opened in 1890. In the northern corner of the park is the Whitworth Art Gallery, which is part of the University of Manchester and is famous for its collection of textiles and wallpapers.

## Stretford

**Left:** Looking south-east towards Manchester Airport, this view shows the green 'urban countryside' of the Mersey valley, with the M60 motorway winding its way towards Stockport. Note the Bridgewater Canal, which was built by the Duke of Bridgewater to facilitate the transportation of coal. Today it is a leisure recourse, bringing holidaymakers into the heart of the city. In the photograph you can see the canal running through Stretford and onwards, under the motorway to Sale on its way to Runcorn. Alongside the canal is the Metrolink line taking busy commuters to work: the old and the new side by side.

**Above:** Looking east across Stretford towards Whalley Range and Chorlton-cum-Hardy.

**Pages 34 and 35:** Looking north along Chester Road towards the city centre.

## Whalley Range

**Above:** In the foreground running left to right is Withington Road, with College Road running top to bottom past the now empty GMB College, where a generation of Union activists were trained. Whalley Range was one of the first well-to-do suburbs of Manchester to appear after the city expanded during the Industrial Revolution. The area was laid out by Victorian property developer Samuel Brookes according to his vision, and many of the original 19th-century buildings remain. There is currently a booming property market in the area, and to halt the demolition of many of the larger houses the suburb was made a conservation area in 1991.

**Right:** A close-up of the area between Withington Road and Alexandra Road South, with the renaissance-style St Bede's College at the top right.

Education

## The University of Manchester

With over 35,000 students on its books, Manchester University is one of the largest in the UK. Formerly called the Victoria University of Manchester, it was merged with the University of Manchester Institute of Science and Technology (UMIST) in 2004. Ernest Rutherford began his research here which lead to the splitting of the atom, and it was here that the world's first programmable computer was built in 1948 by Tom Kilburn and Sir Freddie Williams. Twenty Nobel prize winners have studied or worked at the university over the years.

**Pages 38 and 39:** Salford University campus.

**Above:** Manchester Metropolitan University.
**Left:** The North Campus, formerly UMIST.

## Salford University

The University of Salford can trace its roots back to 1896, when the Salford Working Men's College merged with the Pendleton Mechanics Institute to form the Salford Technical Institute. The original courses of mathematics, engineering, physics, building, chemistry, dyeing, spinning and weaving, and art reflected the industrialisation of 19th-century Salford and Manchester.

The University has over 18,000 students enrolled and more than 2,500 staff and is currently undergoing a £130 million program of construction and upgrading, which includes new buildings for the faculty of health and social care and a flagship new centre for arts and media students.

## Chetham's School of Music

The famous Chetham's School of Music is the largest specialist music school in the UK and is situated within a remarkable collection of buildings, some of which date back to mediaeval times. The school was established in 1969 on the site of Chetham's Hospital. The buildings to the right of the photograph, which include the Baronial Hall and Cloisters, were constructed in the 15th century.

Chetham's Library has been collecting works since the mid-17th century. The large building in the centre of the image was originally built for the Manchester Grammar School in the late 19th century. The small building towards the top of the image is the Vallins Art Centre which was designed by architect Alfred Waterhouse, who also designed the Town Hall, University Quadrangle and nearby Strangeways Prison.

Architecture

**Above:** The Manchester Civil Justice Centre. It is the UK's largest post-19th century court complex and contains 47 court rooms. Designed by Denton Corker Marshall, it is best known for its 'filing cabinet' architectural style.

**Right and Overleaf:** Beetham Tower is the tallest mixed-use building in the United Kingdom and is the highest residential building in Western Europe. Designed by architect Ian Simpson, at 171 metres and 48 storeys it is the UK's tallest building outside of London. The tower includes 219 apartments and a five-star hotel and is notable for its extremely slender design. The upper residential portion of the tower is marked by a step where the upper floors are built out four metres wider than the lower floors. Another feature is the 'Blade' on the roof, which is intended to visually blend the building into the sky.

**Previous page:** Piccadilly

## The Fish Market

**Above:** The old Fish Market in Manchester's Northern Quarter lost its roof long ago, and now only the outer walls of the original building remain. The site has recently been redeveloped to provide mixed urban living spaces and commercial opportunities with new buildings constructed within the preserved and listed original perimeter wall.

## Bridgewater Hall

**Left:** The concert hall, designed by RHWL Architects, opended in 1996 and is noted not just for its stunning architecture but also for its excellent acoustics. The hall is home to both the Hallé and BBC Philharmonic Orchestras and also hosts a wide variety of performances from jazz to pop. In 1998 it won the Civic Trust Special Award for the new building that has done the most to enhance the appearance of a city centre.

## CIS Building

When it was opened in 1962, the CIS building was the third-tallest in Europe and remained the tallest in the UK outside London for 40 years. The concrete service section of the tower was recently re-clad in solar panels to make this one of Manchester's greenest buildings.

## Portland Tower

Also completed in 1962, the Portland Tower was designed by Leach Rhodes Walker. The tower is 80 metres high and has some 21 floors; however, this is now dwarfed by the current crop of skyscrapers such as the Beetham Tower and the proposed 188-metre, 60-storey Inacity Tower.

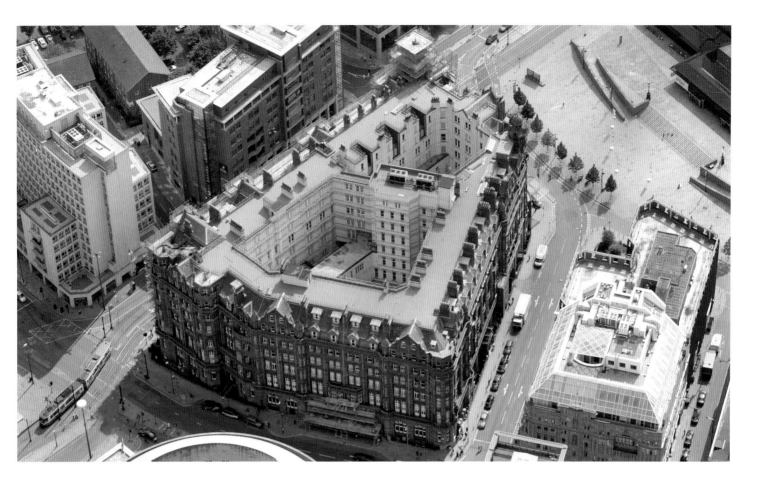

## The Midland Hotel
**Above:** The hotel is famous for being the place where Mr Rolls met Mr Royce, leading to the formation of the Rolls-Royce motor company. It was designed by Charles Trubshaw for the Midland Railway Company and completed in 1903. It offers 303 bedrooms and 14 luxury suites with two restaurants, including a double AA rosette award-winning French restaurant.

## Crown Court
**Left:** The Grade II listed, Gothic-revival style Crown Court on Minshull Street was built between 1867 and 1873 to a design by Thomas Worthington. The building has recently been upgraded by Hurd Rolland Architects with new courts and a glazed atrium over the old courtyard to link all the courts together.

**Above:** Skyline Central, which was completed in 2007, is one of Manchester's newest apartment developments. Behind the long window on the top floor is the private indoor swimming pool.

## GMEX

**Right:** Built in 1880 as Manchester's Central Station by the Cheshire Lines railway, the station served the LNER, LMS and later British Rail until the trains finally ceased to run in May 1969. The 200ft-wide glass roof originally covered six platforms and nine railway tracks. Following a tragic period where is served as a car park, the site was then transformed into the GMEX exhibition centre. Now the single-span roof provides an undivided 7,500sq m exhibition space, which is also used as a concert and sporting venue. Adjacent and connected to it is the new Manchester International Convention Centre.

## The Great Northern Railway Company's Goods Warehouse

The Grade II listed Great Northern Warehouse was built in 1899 by a team of 800 men to a design by W. T. Foxlee. It employed 350 men and offered a next-day delivery service to any station in Britain. The warehouse was built over the top of the underground Manchester and Salford Junction Canal, which had been cut in two by the building of Central Station. However, shafts were sunk beneath the warehouse and the canal was then reused for barge loading and unloading. The canal became disused in 1922, but during World War Two it was drained and used as an air-raid shelter. The underground canal is there to this day and is a piece of Manchester's history that remains hidden. The warehouse itself became disused in 1963 but was then rebuilt and converted to house shops, bars, cafés and a car park.

**Left:** The Abito Apartments, Greengate, a new concept in mini apartments, was designed by BDP and was part of a redevelopment of the Greengate area near the MEN Arena.

## MEN Arena

The *Manchester Evening News* Arena, opened in 1995, is Europe's largest indoor concert venue. Originally built with the year 2000 Olympics bid in mind, it has since proved a huge success as a concert and event venue, with more than a million people visiting during its first year alone. In 2001 it won the Pollstar award for 'International Venue of the Year', and in 2003–04 it won the world's busiest arena venue award, based on concert-ticket sales. A series of concerts by the band Take That were seen by 140,000 people and 84,000 came to see Kylie Minogue. Other events included concerts by Madonna, Sir Paul McCartney, Pavarotti and The Rolling Stones. Sporting events hosted at the arena have included football, ice hockey and boxing, and it was used in the 2002 Commonwealth Games.

**Right:** The Albert Memorial, which was built to remember Prince Albert of Saxe-Coburg and Gotha, Prince Consort to Queen Victoria, after he died in 1861 at the age of just 42.

## Spinningfields

Spinningfields is Manchester's new business district comprising a number of mixed-use landmark buildings. In the foreground the white building is Manchester's first skyscraper, Sunlight House, and then behind it to the right is the new offices of the *Manchester Evening News* . The M.E.N. was started as an election sheet in 1868 by prospective MP Mitchell Henry. After the election it was taken over by Peter Allen and John Edward Taylor, who developed it, and it continued to grow until, by 1939, it was the largest regional newspaper in Britain. Today it continues to develop and now owns the *Metro News*, Britain's widest-circulating free newspaper, and is working on new multimedia ventures including a Manchester TV channel.

## Victoria Baths

Victoria Baths was opened on 7 September 1906. Designed by Henry Price, who was Manchester's first city architect, the baths included three pools, a laundry and a Turkish bath. No expense was spared on the building, which was beautifully clad in brick and terracotta with stained-glass windows on the outside and ceramic tiles on the inside. In 1952 Britain's first public jacuzzi was installed. However, the baths then fell into decline and were closed in 1993. Since then there has been a strongly backed campaign to restore the building to its former glory, and after winning BBC2's *Restoration* competition it looks well on the way to success.

## Oxford Road

Here we see the junction of Whitworth Street West and Oxford Road, with the trendy new apartments on the corner contrasting with the apparently tiny Ritz dance hall next door. On the right and in the close-up photograph we can see the Baroque Portland Stone façade of the Grade II listed St James Building by Clegg, Fryer & Penman from 1912, originally commissioned by the Calico Printers' Association and now home to numerous businesses. An interesting survivor of times gone by is the tiny yellow Peveril of the Peak pub in the upper-left of the above image. On the station approach is the famous Cornerhouse Cinema and Art Gallery.

## Chimney Pot Park, Salford
**Above:** This fascinating development by Urban Splash takes traditional terraced housing and turns it on its head. Literally, in fact, as the houses now have the bedrooms on the lower floor allowing a larger living space and terrace upstairs. As you can see, in the row in the lower right, the houses are gutted and then completely rebuilt, retaining the character of the old terraces while providing the functionality of modern homes.

## Piccadilly Gardens
**Left:** Recently remodelled, the gardens feature a walkway through an interactive fountain and a café pavilion by Japanese architect Tadao Ando, designed to shield the gardens from the hubbub of the neighbouring transport interchange. Although entirely renewed, the gardens still contain one link with the past: the 1901 Queen Victoria memorial by Edward Onslow Ford.

**Royal Exchange**

Above: Originally built as a cotton exchange, the Royal Exchange now contains shops and the Royal Exchange Theatre, which was founded by a group of artistic directors in 1968. As well as traditional works, the theatre is strongly supportive of new projects.

**Palace Hotel**

Right: Originally the Refuge Assurance building, it was converted to a hotel in 1996. The building is another work by Sir Alfred Waterhouse and his son Paul. Opened in 1910, the brick and terracotta building is Grade II listed.

## Chorlton Street
**Above:** At the bottom of the image we can see MMUBS, the Manchester Metropolitan University Business School, and running up the centre of the image towards Portland Tower is Chorlton Street in the heart of the nightlife area with its cafés and bars. Slightly to the left is Sackville Park, notable as the location of the statue of Alan Turing, the computer pioneer.

## Manchester Metropolitan University Hollings Campus – the toast-rack
**Left:** Known locally as 'the toast-rack', the Hollings College was designed by L.C. Howitt and opened in 1960. The adjoining circular building is known as 'the fried egg'. The buildings were Grade II listed in 1998. Originally a catering college, it now caters for fashion as well as food.

### Manchester Town Hall

Opened in 1887, the Gothic revival town hall was Alfred Waterhouse's masterpiece. It cost a million pounds to build and was lavishly decorated with statues and carvings of important Mancunian figures, including General Agricola, the founder of the original Roman fort of Mamuciam. The town hall is notable for its 85m-tall clock tower and also a series of 12 frescoes by Ford Madox Brown. In front of the town hall is Albert Square, and prominent in the photograph is the memorial to Prince Albert of Saxe-Coburg and Gotha, who would no doubt feel very at home during the regular German markets held in the square.

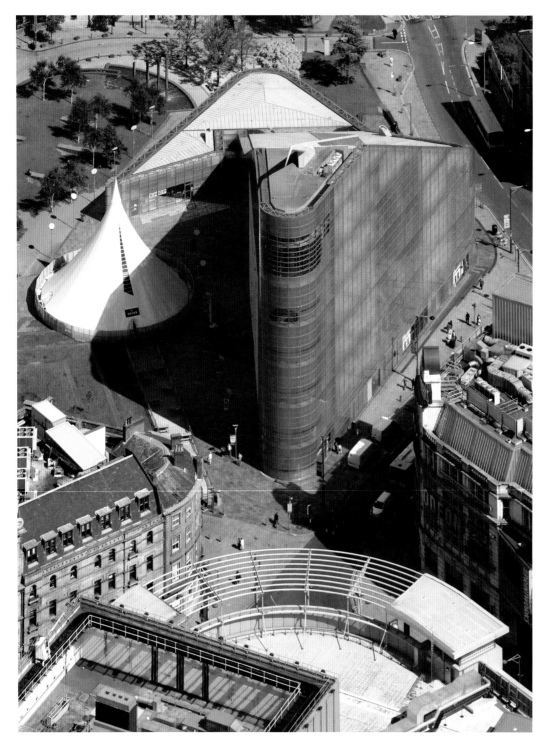

## URBIS

Situated in Cathedral Gardens, central Manchester, Urbis offers a 'dynamic programme of changing exhibitions offering unique insights into the culture of the modern city, with innovative explorations of design, architecture, graffiti, music and the urban environment'. It is also home to Channel M, the Manchester TV channel.

The building, opened in 2002, was designed by Ian Simpson and cost £30 million.

**Pages 78 and 79:** Urbis and the triangle.

Commerce

## Canal Street

**Above:** Along the bank of the Rochdale Canal lies Canal Street. Once an area of derelict warehouses, it has now been transformed into a centrepiece of trendy cafés, bars and clubs. The Rochdale Canal was opened in 1804 to connect the Bridgewater Canal with Rochdale and beyond as far as Sowerby Bridge. The canal fell into disuse in the 20th century and most of it was closed in 1952. However, it has recently undergone extensive restoration and by 2002 the canal was again fully navigable.

## Mosley Street

**Right:** The heart of the financial district, the area in and around Mosley Street contains some wonderful architectural gems, such as the Portico Library (1806), the Bradford and Bingley building, the Royal Bank of Scotland (1862), the Midland bank (1935) designed by Sir Edwin Lutyens, on Kings Street, and the wonderfully Baroque Parrs Bank (1902).

## Trafford Park

Trafford Park is the world's first and biggest industrial park, created in 1896 when the De Trafford family sold the estate to Trafford Park Estates. Originally a park, the area's location adjacent to the Manchester Ship Canal made it ideal for industrial development, and although the docks have now closed the adjacent motorways link the park with the modern transport system. Many famous names have moved here over the years, including Hovis in 1914, Kellogs in 1938 and the Westinghouse Electric company (later Metropolitan Vickers) in 1899. My grandfather built Model T Fords here, and it was here that a Mr Allcock met a Mr Brown at the Vickers plant to plan the first transatlantic flight in 1919.

### The Northern Quarter

Mancunians have always had a strong entrepreneurial spirit, and this shows strongly today in the city's Northern Quarter, with its multitude of small businesses. The area has not had the same level of renewal as other parts of the city, but this has allowed the area to retain its own individual character, a character of small and medium businesses often catering for more unusual niche markets. There are some 610 businesses in the M4 area, with a strong presence from creative businesses such as designers, architects and marketing firms.

Retail

## The Arndale Centre

When it was completed in 1979, the Manchester Arndale Centre, with over 200 shops, was Europe's largest enclosed shopping centre. The centre was designed by architects Hugh Wilson and Lewis Womersley, and it has recently been modernised with a new glass and steel entrance to Exchange Square and a new glass-roofed Winter Garden.

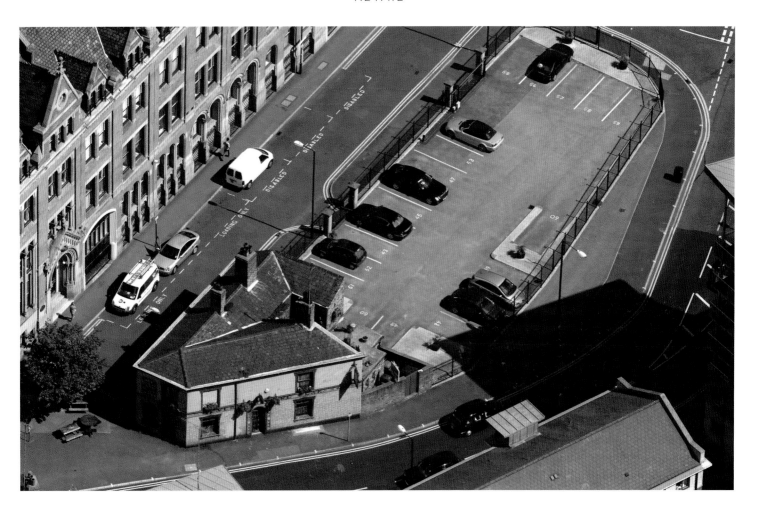

**The Peveril of the Peak.**
**Above:** This Grade II listed pub dates from the early 19th Century and is reputed to be haunted!

**The Manchester Wheel**
**Left:** With 42 Carriages, lit by 51,000 bulbs and 60 meters high, this big wheel is one of the largest mobile big wheels in the world. It was first seen at the Champs Elysees, Paris, for the millennium, where it sported a leather VIP carriage for President Jaques Chirac. A number of these wheels have been built by Nauta-Bussink in the Netherlands, and the wheel was first brought to Manchester as a temporary attraction for Christmas 2004. The wheel was dismantled afterwards but was so popular it was brought back several times afterwards. The wheel is not permanently anchored, instead it is ballasted by 40,000 litres of water to aid easy removal.

## Deansgate

**Above:** One of Manchester's main shopping streets with its most prestigious store, Kendals, visible in the centre of the image.

## The Triangle

**Right:** Formerly the Corn Exchange, the Triangle, built between 1897 and 1903, has recently been remodelled with major structural alterations to the interior, to become a first-class shopping arcade. There had been a produce market on the site since mediaeval times, and the design by architects Ball and Else is notable for its iron and glass-domed roof. In modern times it has become notable for the giant TV screen on its exterior wall. The building lies within the Cathedral Conservation Area, which was created in 1972.

## Stretford Shopping Centre

**Above:** The former Stretford Arndale Centre was built as one of a string of 18 Arndale shopping centres around the UK. Set up by Arnold Hagenbach and Sam Chippindale, after whom they were named, these were the country's first American mall-style shopping centres.

## M&S

**Left:** It was in Manchester that Marks and Spencer set up their first store, and today their new flagship store is situated not far from the original Cheetham site. The store has been built from scratch, involving the demolition of the previous nine-storey building on the site. It is the largest M&S store in the world, with over 23,500sq m of floorspace. Designed by Building Design Partnership and built by Bovis, the new structure is walled in glass with a glass tube walkway connecting it to the adjacent Arndale Centre.

**Overleaf:** The Trafford Centre.

Sport

## Sport in Manchester

Manchester has always had a strong sporting tradition, right from grass-roots up to the very top levels of sports. The city has a whole host of sporting facilities, including two top football stadiums, the National Squash Centre and the Manchester Aquatics Centre. The City hosted the 2002 Commonwealth Games, for which many of these facilities were constructed. Above is Woodhouses Cricket Club and right is the Power League Five-a-Side Soccer Centre in Ardwick.

## Manchester Velodrome
**Above:** Home to the British Cycling Team, the Manchester Velodrome is the National Cycling Centre and Britain's best indoor Olympic cycle track. Purpose-built for the 2002 Commonwealth Games, the centre is one of the world's fastest. The World Track Championships were held here in 1996 and 2000.

## The XVII Commonwealth Games
**Left:** The 2002 Commonwealth Games was the biggest multi-sport event to be held in Britain since the 1948 Olympic Games. The games involved 14 individual and three team sports, with athletes competing from 72 countries. The City of Manchester Stadium was built especially for the event and was later reconfigured to serve as the home of Manchester City Football Club.

**Above:** The Willows Stadium, home of Salford City Reds Rugby League Team. Opened in 1901 there are now plans for a new stadium to be built at Barton.

## Old Trafford Cricket Ground

**Right:** Established in 1857, and hosting Test Matches since 1884, this is the home of the Lancashire County Cricket Club and has a capacity of 22,000. Highlights include when Jim Laker was the first to take all 10 wickets in the Test Match against Australia in 1956 and the 1999 World Cup when India played Pakistan in front of a packed venue. The ground has also hosted non-cricketing events such as music concerts.

## Trafford Water Sport Centre

Situated in the south of Manchester, the 45-acre lake is used for sailing, angling, windsurfing, kayaking, powerboating and model boating. The centre was opened in 1980, using the lake created by a flooded gravel quarry which had been used to build the adjacent M60 motorway in 1972. The lake and surrounding Mersey Valley are home to a great variety of wildlife, and there is a visitors' centre which details that wildlife visible in the top-right corner of the photograph.

## Chill Factor E

**Above:** Manchester's newest sporting facility is Chill Factor E, the UK's biggest indoor ski slope.

## The City of Manchester Stadium

**Right:** Designed by Arup and built by Laing for the Commonwealth Games in 2002, at a cost of £110 million, the stadium was then reconfigured for football by lowering the pitch 10 metres and adding a lower level of seating. The Northern Stand was also completed and roofed over. The stadium has a capacity of 47,000 for football and even more when it is used for concerts. The area around the stadium is known as Sportcity, which includes the adjacent Regional Athletics Arena, the National Squash Centre and the Velodrome.

## Old Trafford

Manchester's most famous building, and home to arguably the world's most famous football club, Manchester United. The club was formed in 1878 as the Newton Heath, Lancashire and Yorkshire Railway football club. The Old Trafford stadium, also known as the 'Theatre of Dreams', has been the home of the club since 1910, and with a capacity of 76,000 it is the second largest stadium in Britain after the new Wembley Stadium. In 2006 the North Stand corners were filled in to add 9,000 seats to the capacity. Further enlargement to the south is hindered by the railway line, although the lower roof level of the south side lends itself to aerial photographs of the stadium.

Transport

## Piccadilly

The areas around the junction of the Ashton Canal and Rochdale Canal at Piccadilly have seen a lot of changes over the years, from industrial boom in the 18th and 19th centuries to the decline in the late 20th century and now back to boom with the current regeneration. The close-up above shows the new Paradise Wharf development, and much of the remaining open space in these images is about to be reconstructed. There are plans for a 188-metre/58-storey tower called Inacity Tower, which will be built on the car park to the right foreground of the image on the left.

**Pages 114 and 115:** The Bridgewater Canal in the Castlefield conservation area.

## Hulme Arch

**Above:** Princess Road as it passes under the new 25 metre-high Hulme Arch, which carries Stretford Road, suspended by means of ranked spiral steel cables.

## Inner ring road

**Right:** Manchester has two ring roads: the outer is the M60 motorway and the inner can be seen in this view from the south. The section on the right is the Mancunian Way, which was the region's first urban motorway taking traffic from industrial east Manchester to the docks in the west. It was opened by Harold Wilson in 1967. Also in the image we can see the extensive transport infrastructure of the city from the River Irwell, the Bridgewater Canal, the Rochdale Canal and the railways, which have been updated with the new metrolink light rail system.

## Thomas Telford Basin

**Above:** The Thomas Telford Basin is part of the Ashton Canal, which opened in 1796 and links Manchester with Ashton-under-Lyne. It also connects to the Huddersfield Narrow and Peak Forest Canals and forms part of the Cheshire ring. The Ashton Canal fell into disrepair in the mid-20th century, but in 1972–74 it was cleared and reopened by a group of 1,000 volunteers and now serves as an important leisure resource.

## Merchants Bridge

**Left:** Not all Manchester's Canal infrastructure dates from the 18th or 19th century: Merchants Bridge was built in 1995 to cross the Bridgewater Canal and link Slate Wharf and Catalan Square in the Castlefield conservation area. This striking Sickle Arch bridge, designed by RHWL, is constructed of tubular steel and was assembled on the canal bank and then lifted into position by a huge crane.

**Previous page:** The old and the new side by side; the M602 Motorway and the Manchester Ship canal both passing through Eccles on their way to the city centre.

**Left:** Manchester's newest canal is this branch built as part of the New Islington Millennium Community project.

### New East Manchester Gateway

**Right and overleaf:** Built at a cost of £36.5 million, the New East Manchester Gateway comprises the Gateway Road, the new Metrolink station with its unique copper canopy and the 4,000-ton Finback Bridge, which will carry the Oldham/Rochdale Metrolink extension. The gateway forms a bus/road/rail interchange to serve the new Central Park development, which is bringing high technology employment to the area.

## Oxford Road Station

**Above:** Oxford Road Station is noted for its unusual architecture, and it was built to replace the old Victorian buildings in 1960 when the line was upgraded and electrified. The roof was originally constructed with three conoidal laminated wood shells, reminiscent of the Sydney Opera House.

## Piccadilly Station

**Left:** The biggest and the busiest station in Manchester with 14 platforms, it is also a terminus for the Metrolink trams. Originally called London Road Station, it was opened in 1842 as the terminus of the Manchester and Birmingham Railway. The station buildings were rebuilt in 1969 and then remodelled again for the 2002 Commonwealth Games. In the background on the right the little-known and short-lived Mayfield Station can just be seen, which was built in 1910 and closed in 1960.

**Railway Depot**
Opened in May 2006, this new £30 million train maintenance depot was built to service the new fleet of 185 Pennine Class trains entering service with First TransPennine Express. The fleet of 51 Diesel Multiple Unit trains was built by Siemens at a cost of £200 million and are capable of speeds of 100mph.

## Victoria Station

The original building was designed by George Stephenson and opened as the Hunts Bank Station in 1844, with just a single platform to serve the Manchester & Leeds Railway. This grew, and by the late 19th century it was one of the biggest stations in Britain. The distinctive Edwardian frontage was built in 1902, and the station has now been integrated into the Metrolink System and also serves as the terminus for the adjacent MEN Arena.

**Salford Quays**

Opened in 1894 by Queen Victoria, the Manchester Ship Canal was built to link the docks at Salford Quays to the sea. This allowed Manchester to become Britain's third-largest port and helped the industrialisation of the city. By the 1970s, however, many ships were too big for the canal, and the docks eventually closed in 1982. Since then the area has been regenerated and transformed with new infrastructures such as the Metrolink trams and the cultural icons of the Lowry Gallery and Imperial War Museum North. The Detroit Bridge (right) was originally a railway swing bridge which linked Salford to Trafford, but it was later relocated here to provide a footbridge over the Huron and Erie Basins.

**Overleaf:** Salford Quays.

**Liverpool Road Station**
**Above:** Opened in 1830, this was the world's first passenger Railway Station and formed the terminus for the Liverpool & Manchester Railway, the one which the famous Rainhill trials were held at to select Stephenson's Rocket as the locomotive. In 1844 the station was replaced for passengers by Victoria Station but continued to be used for freight until 1975. It has now been restored to its 1830 condition and forms the basis of the Museum of Science & Industry.

**Left:** Salford Quays.

## Old Trafford Road Bridge

**Above:** At 1,800 tons this is the heaviest swing bridge in the UK and was recently rebuilt so that it no longer swings, although the control tower remains next to it as a monument to times gone by.

## Barton Swing Bridge

**Right:** One of the wonders of the industrial age, the aqueduct opened in 1893 and was built to carry the Bridgewater Canal over the Ship Canal. It swings open along with the adjacent road swing bridge to allow larger ships to pass up the canal. This is accomplished by closing hydraulic sealing doors which seal the water in the bridge and at both ends of the canal, allowing the bridge to swing while containing 800 tons of water.

## Swinton Interchange

One of the reasons for the success of Manchester over the years has been the city's excellent transport infrastructure from canals to railways and now motorways and airports. The Swinton interchange forms the junction between the M62 to Liverpool, the M602 to Salford and the city centre and the M60 orbital ring road. The adjacent Barton Bridge was the first bit of the M60 to be opened, but it took another 40 years before the orbital was completed in 2000.

Culture

## The BBC

Situated on Oxford Road and opened in 1975, the New Broadcasting House produces many local TV programmes and BBC Radio Manchester is broadcast from here via a transmitter on Holme Moss. The future of the building is uncertain at the moment as the BBC will be relocating to the new Media City being constructed at Salford Quays (above).

## The Street

Right in the heart of Manchester are the Granada TV studios, and here we can see the set of its most famous programme, *Coronation Street*. Based on a real street in Salford called Archie Street, the first set was indoors and scaled down, but in 1982 this full-sized outdoor version was built, although most of the interior scenes are still shot in the adjoining indoor studio. The neighbouring rows of houses and passing Metrolink tram shown in the programme's opening credits are in fact computer-generated special effects.

## Manchester Cathedral

Much of what we see today dates from the 19th century when the cathedral was restored by Joseph Crowther; however, parts of the tower base date back to 1380. The cathedral is sited in the original mediaeval village centre, and a St Mary's Church was mentioned in the Domesday Book and may well have stood on the same site. In 1421 the church became a Collegiate Foundation, dedicated to St Mary, St Denys and St George, becoming a cathedral in 1847. The church was ransacked during the English Civil War in 1649 and suffered bomb damage during World War Two.

## St Mary's in Hulme

**Above:** With the tallest spire in Manchester at a height of 242ft , St Mary's is about to be converted into an unusual home with seven floors. The Grade II listed church was originally built in 1858 to a design by J.S.Crowther.

## Castlefield Church

**Right:** Built in 1856 to a design by Edward Walter, the former Congregational Chapel is now a recording studio. To the left of the Congregational Chapel the remains of Manchester's first Canal Warehouse, the Grocers Warehouse, can be seen, designed by James Brindley and built in around 1775. Unfortunately it was demolished in 1960.

### Castlefield Open Air Theatre

**Above:** Located in the Giants Basin on the Bridgewater Canal in the Castlefield conservation area, the outdoor arena plays host to a huge variety of events. The canopy is permanently in place allowing impromptu gatherings as well as formal shows. Big screens have also occasionally been set up to show major sporting events such as the 2006 Football World Cup.

**Right:** Central Library.

### Central Library

Following the Public Libraries and Museums Act of 1850, Manchester was the first authority to set up a free lending library in 1852 in the Hall of Science, located where the Science & Industry Museum is now. Construction of a purpose-built library, to a design by E. Vincent Harris, began in 1930 with a foundation laid by Prime Minister Ramsey McDonald. The building has a classical exterior style but was built with a modern steel frame inside, and it was opened in 1934 by King George V.

## The Imperial War Museum North

Opened in 2002 and designed by the world-famous architect Daniel Libeskind, the 6,000sq m steel and aluminium building is designed to represent a globe shattered by war into 'shards'. The 'shards' represent the three elements in which war is fought: the main display area is the Earth Shard, the restaurant area is the Water Shard and the tower is the Air Shard. The museum contains exhibits covering various periods of history, with an emphasis on the effect of war on ordinary people.

## The Lowry

Opened in 2000, the Lowry spearheaded the regeneration of the Salford Quays area. The gallery houses many works by local artist Laurence Stephen Lowry, after whom the building takes its name. There is a large collection of work by other artists from various styles and periods, as well as two theatres. Designed by Michael Wilford, the building required 48,000 tons of concrete, 5,263sq m of glass and 2,466 tons of steel to build it and, together with the adjacent plaza and lifting footbridge, cost £106 million.

**Pages 158 and 159:** The Lowry and the Salford Quays lifting footbridge.

## Manchester Art Gallery

Acquired by the Manchester Corporation in 1882, the gallery has recently had a four-year and £35 million redevelopment, which included an adjoining new building by Michael Hopkins and Partners. The gallery now has 2,500sq m of display space to show the 25,000 items in its collection of fine art, decorative art and costume. With the help of the Contemporary Art Society, the gallery has also acquired a collection of contemporary furniture, sculpture and photography.

## The Roman Fort

The Roman General Julius Agricola settled in Manchester in AD 79, building his fort on a hill overlooking the confluence of the Rivers Medlock and Irwell. The Roman name 'Mamuciam' derives from this location and translates as 'breast-shaped hill'. The site was chosen as a defensible location on a strategic hub of the routes between Roman settlements in York, Chester, Wigan, Ribchester and Middlewich. The fort went through several stages of development and was used right up until the end of the Roman occupation in AD 410. The reconstruction we see today is built on the original foundations and shows the fort as it would have looked in around AD 200.

## Manchester Museum

The Manchester Museum collection started with the private collection of John Leigh Philips (1761–1814). In 1821, after his death, the Manchester Natural History Society was formed to take over the collection. In 1868 the collection was transferred to the University of Manchester, or Owens College as it was known at the time. The society then commissioned Alfred Waterhouse to design the magnificent Gothic structure we see today, and the museum was opened in 1890. It contains a wide range of exhibits and is particularly noted for its Egyptology collection.

**St Ann's**
**Above:** Built in a cornfield in 1712, when Manchester was just a small country village, St Ann's was only Manchester's second church after what is now the cathedral. St Ann's Square was laid out in 1720 when Manchester was starting to grow as it headed into the Industrial Revolution.

**St Peter's Square**
**Left:** The square was originally the site of St Peter's Church, which stood here from 1788 to 1907. The Cenotaph was erected in 1924 to a design by Edward Lutyens and is a near replica of the one in London.